LONGING DISTANCE

Poems of Love, Lust & Geography

Joanie Puma

Finishing Line Press
Georgetown, Kentucky

LONGING DISTANCE

Poems of Love, Lust & Geography

ACKNOWLEDGMENTS

Thanks to Elizabeth Macklin and to William Stafford's "The Little Girl by the
Fence at School."

Publisher: Leah Maines

Editor: Christen Kincaid

Cover Art: Author's collection

Author Photo: Allison Jeffrey

Cover Design: Elizabeth Maines McCleavy

Printed in the USA on acid-free paper.
Order online: www.finishinglinepress.com
              also available on amazon.com

Author inquiries and mail orders:
Finishing Line Press
P. O. Box 1626
Georgetown, Kentucky 40324
U. S. A.

Table of Contents

For my parents

BEFORE THE LOVE STATE

did I always break down on Tuesdays?
Was I always so kind to bugs of every stripe?
Have I always jabbered to supermarket cashiers,
gas-station attendants and waved to
kids on bikes from mine?

The colors of the world, the soft grass
backyard undertow, even the sinfully
lusciously summery air, too dry,
too smoky this combustible year,
possess a comfortable ordinariness,
but something is different.

It goes deeper down, the vibrations of
life having been altered somehow
so in that ordinary comfort resides
some kind of pervasive invisible glow
so that events act to make my life sweet,
even when I remember to miss you.

My life divides into two parts: now and
before the love state. I didn't zero
in and call it the love state
until, dyslexic, I misread a line
in a poem by that good Irish poet.

But it's true:
I, too, sat up before the stove late
before the love state.

LOOKING FOR JOAN BAEZ'S MAILBOX

We crept along the highway through Big Sur,
eyes peeled for any sign of Joan Baez's mailbox.
If we found it, could Dylan be very far beyond?
Our methods were unquestioned, unmocked,
encouraged, imitated by our friend
driving us in his new Volkswagen
bigger bug with high-back seats.

One weekend in the Catskills, it took two tankfuls
of regular to prowl past Shady and Pine Hill, lurch
under Overlook Mountain, all over Ulster County.
We slowed to stare at faces. Sometimes we thought
we heard Paul Butterfield's voice or his harmonica.
If we could hear it, could Dylan be far beyond?

In the late-mid-60s we walked under open Village
windows wafting voices and guitar notes—
we looked up hungrily—how could we get in?—
who were they up there?
Were we going to browse through life
or someday would we create a world and
live in it, too?

ENGULF COAST

It took—still takes—ten minutes
to escape familial
kudzu: I don't realize
at first that's what I'm doing—
I just want to get outside.
I rush for the door, careful
not to slam it—don't want to
piss anybody off—it's
tense enough already. I
seat myself on the front steps,
chin on hands, elbows on knees
between carefully clipped shrubs,
watch the sun slide down steep clouds
that become mountains, fjords,
amid a stillness so great,
I'm not there, not anywhere,
far from the din of my roots.
Deep-breath-nourishment stillness,
concrete steps so warm and soft.

THE HOUSE AROUND THE CORNER

smothered me in blinds-drawn-dark mid-afternoon,
the stale-smelling, stuffy air, blue
kitchen linoleum, blue vinyl-and-stainless
lazy-S'd chairs, chugging, vapor-emitting icebox,
sombre Austro-Hungarian-accented "Thank you, dahling,"
as I handed her the sweating glass of ice water.

Floor-to-ceiling piles of pulp sci-fi paperbacks
the youngest—the most brilliant, the most scattered—
collected well into his nervous, smiling fifties;
their covers, heroic-comic-book realism,
nordic-jawed heroes oppose bullet-buxomed
blonde and brunette warrioresses.

Stacks of sheet music, "I've Got a Lovely Bunch
of Coconuts," "Whispering," "Music, Music, Music"—
there was fighting, fighting, fighting—the oldest, most
bitter, most resentful, left atop the old upright
he banged on, fingers straight out and stiff
to hide his feeling and delicacy.

Deserter, pariah in the eyes of my grandma and
two maiden uncles, my mother had had the nerve
to get married—it took nerve to stay or leave—
she had too much or too little. No longer
privy to the inner circle in quite the same way,
moving us 2,000 miles, anyway, in pursuit of it.

The chair at the head of the long living room,
winged seat of power with tiny embroidered footstool;
sometimes I dared to light on the edge, my legs still
bearing most of my weight, for the rare seconds she left it
to inspect gladiolas out back where her sons grew
them for her to cradle like scepters or spears.

The imagery was there the whole time, but we just
went about our business, carrying trays of hot meats,

chickens and vegetables and potato and noodle pudding,
cold salads and fruits, covered with brown grocery bags,
in and out of the car, Dad driving the 300 yards as carefully
as he endured patiently the drama he stumbled in on.

Many angry words clung to those transient dinners when
surely all anybody really meant to say was "I love you."
And all the while Mother played at dutiful daughter, faithful wife,
good mother, maybe all she really wanted was to be a little girl
like me, on the periphery, squinting in the harsh light,
my grandmother in her chair, the four adults playing cards.

WHAT I WAS FEELING

A strange young woman knocked
at the door of the Victorian house
in Flushing, Queens at nine o'clock
on a Sunday night in the mid-seventies,
asked to borrow a knife of all things,
and the shock and fear and confusion
that rose in me because I watch the news
was instantly muffled by good manners
as I stood there enclosed in the foyer,
the screen door to the porch still locked,
the door closed behind me to the parlor.

Inside, my dog pawed wildly,
scratched violently, nosed fruitlessly,
trying to get the door to me open,
trying to get to the other
side of the door where I was
camouflaged by my skin,
a six-inch-thick wall,
and crummy modern instincts.

"What's going on?" my husband asked looking up from his paper.

DOMESTICITY

You stood next to me,
bits of colored paper shavings in your hands,
complaints about your job in your mouth—
you didn't like people telling you what to do.

You stepped around me to the stove and
dropped the pellets into a pan of heating water.
I squinted a question with my face.
"Fireworks," you said. I nodded.
"Hand me some more," you said. I didn't know.
"Are you telling me what to do?" Not exactly.
I handed you two anyway, but no more.

We turned from the stove and embraced
each other like Eskimos in a kiss
that made our shoulders, hips, knees
swivel as the water boiled.

SURPRISE

A morning of fast driving
with the windows down across Texas
makes such good time I arrive in mid-afternoon,
some two hours earlier than expected,
which accounts for my new longer hairdo
being windblown and for my father being
roused from his ritual faraway nap
and which surely explains his vacant stare
as he comes to the door, peers through
the latched screen and asks uneasily,
"What do you want?"

EXCITABLE

When the Western wind blows mean blows
I long to be surrounded
by tall, sturdy, wise pines—
long to become one—calmly tilting
in a gale, softly bending branches.
But the prairie tree of choice is cottonwood—
cottonwoods that grow wild and multi-trunked
in the country, pruned in town—sign of
strength, exuberance, water. In the wind,
shushing, hissing, rattling, howling, cottonwoods,
their blinking, blaring, flashy, talky light-bulb leaves
is nature's answer to the Las Vegas strip at night.
My favorite one grows across the street
dark-barked, cropped slender
with the potent massive somber treeness
of a darkly enchanted dragon-infested forest.

The West is too damn distracting:
flat-bed hot-rodders, lawn mowers, mid-morning marching-band
pre-rodeo rehearsals. You throw a tennis ball up to serve—
if the shock of cobalt-blue sky doesn't get you
the little wisps of cottonwood seeds that soar
relentlessly over your head like snowflakes
in a child's crystal toy will trance you out.
The sagging late summer breeze grants these
old-man seedlings shortened trips, they drop
in the grass straightaway. In July they'd dodge
and fly for miles, I couldn't catch even one, but now
in August four have come to rest on my porch,
in my lap, in my hair, on my shirt. I hold them
between thumb and forefinger, feel their pulse,
as the usual clouds—bright glowing ivory white
crisply outlined masses—drift off and give way to
a close sky of noisy undefined cottony gauze.

LAST DATE

We meet on empty, snowy street
squeak the crunching snows of weeks—
too small a town for this many poets,
I know right away it's a dream.

In an ethnic restaurant—
there are none around here—we sit
across from each other. I'm not drawn to him
except to counteract his irritating interest
in the waitress, the woman at the next table.

We talk about *his* work—it's a familiar plot—
lying on the table between us,
a copy of a glistening monthly.
I find his poem and compliment it—
even on imaginary dates
men are jerks, women knee-jerks.

Something strikes me about his poem:
the third stanza recreates the tide
coming in—he's not really that good,
it's a dream, remember—but as
the foam gets thinner and each line
breaks between white caps, I decide
it's a conceit, a trick I want to try.

Finally, he asks, "What excites you?"
I wake up.

MONEY-HUNGRY HARPY HOLDS HIS HEIRLOOMS HOSTAGE

The porcelain sits in a circle of twelve
stacks, one for each year of marriage, dinner
plates on the bottom, on top of them
luncheon plates, followed by the cream
soup bowls with their delicate eared handles,
balanced on top of them saucers then
giant European coffee cups, surrounds
the woman menacingly like a lost chapter
from *Alice in Wonderland* or some obscure
ritual, the Sun Place-Setting Ceremony.
Standing in the center of the carpet,
a radial distance of three feet,
she could form an hour and minute hand
if she got down on her side on the floor with them.

She searched for three months every source:
"I've seen every plate in the city, and these are the
only ones I like." The husband trusted her taste
to embarrassing degrees—no aesthetic of his own
all he wanted was to be stylish.
With relish and relief he sallied
into the Royal Copenhagen store with her—
$112 a place setting forced the ruse of a joint decision.
Such mid-70s-lavish spending would not be stylish now—
it's wise to be ahead of one's time.
Leather couches, art-nouveau oak
rockers, Indian carpets, a regimental oak
officers dining table, six Queen Anne oak
chairs with leather seats, a parquet-floor-in-oak
four-room co-op on Riverside Drive.
Just before the end she spotted
pre-Elizabethan hand-hammered silver
replications with three-tined forks.
She got over it and moved away with
a sensible set of sturdy stainless.

LITTLE WHEELS

A dark-plastic-paneled room lined
with polyester-magenta-clothed folding tables:
where the local royalty takes lunch,
hungry, slit-eyed, grins and chuckles,
their fat-cat chiseler cholesteroled hearts
beat to the song their esteemed membership
warbles before condemning the foreign-exchange
student who broke their rules,
living too fully and in a way they can't
even imagine after which they'll
spit out their toothpicks in the
direction of each other's jugular
and go back to their offices.

THE NEW WEST

Canyons cut by water,
people cut by lack of it:
rocks, boulders worn rounded, smooth,
cowboys, sheepdogs, artistes whet their razor edges,
grind a pulp of doomed pines, sheep, cows, your best self.
Makes you want to take 'em to a subway and
make 'em dance.

RIDING HIGH

The clouds whisk the roof
of my low-slung hatchback,
make me an egomaniac,
my forehead's high as the sky—
seven-some-thousand feet, no
exceptional altitude for a pass
in the West—burning U. S. 191
past Flaming Gorge, over Uintas Mountains,
through Ashley National Forest. I sob
over and over to myself, "Ashley! Ashley!"
I know Ashley Wilkes is not
this forest's namesake. Driving on top
of the world makes me giddy,
or driving since four this morning;
no other cars, my own private Utah.
Uintahs. You-in-taws? Oo-een-tahs?

High up in a city bus down Avenue P,
the roadbed's built up so high, the houses
ebb down and away like a Pacific beach,
horizontally mounted steering wheel
gleamed brown plastic at me, ten years old,
on a bus in America: the indignity of it all.

Bouncing with Jack Slaughter
in his beat-up blue gardening van, towers
over the houses of old new Austin,
beats walking the running path by the river
where we didn't even make eye contact—
he showed up in a sport coat and go-to-meetin' boots,
ogled all those Sunday girls instead of me,
thankful me, forty-six and my eyes aren't dilated yet.

It might come down to two things:
water and riding up high.

THE DAY THE SKY WAS GREEN

some cosmic lightning hurler
pricked my house for target practice
just after the wind began to howl and I
shuddered under an overturned wing chair,
the bolts flying so freely I didn't dare
run to the bigger neighbor house for shelter
or company so I crouched there,
an upholstered human turtle waited it out,
prayed, negative ions illuminated the day,
loose electrons orbited my head.

GETTING LOST

Some people need directions:
bright red blazes on birches
keep you on the path until
a giant's tangle of fallen trees and branches
detour you into the forest
suddenly descending steeply southwest
following rivulets of your own doing.

CROWS

In the quiet early sun I realize
I've forgotten the dutiful phone call,
harbor ill will toward both lapse and duty.
I hear them before I see them
suddenly burst out of a blue spruce so
close to my head I feel like Tippy Hedron.
Behavior adjusters, karmic schoolmarms—
does everything have to be a sign?—
alarm my heart, my conscience:
no bible, torah, mahabharata, tao
could have made me duck lower.

FALLING INTO EAGLE LAKE, BOOTS AND ALL

Like Camille fragile and coughing
the forest whispers, "I vahnt to be alone,"
and it will be soon after
the last tourist goes home.

I'm not leaving yet, I just got here,
the Princess Di suite, its angled inside-out
Mansard-ish pine-covered ceiling,
salivatable square footage I won in a drawing—
I stare across the lake at flashes of color sent
from mixed hardwoods, listen for loons, a coyote,
the last motorboat, the dinner bell.

Soon there will be quiet snowflakes,
sleeping spruces, canoes in storage, lake on ice;
clouds chug coyly behind the Harvest/Bull Moon.
I stand in the lawn,
dew turning into frost around my feet.

AT ONE WITH BUDDHA AND BUGS IN THE MOONLIGHT

I walk with Buddha and Bugs through
blue moonlit fog, leaves crackle, fall on each
other, deer too quiet or we're too noisy
on architecture, axe murderers, cats.

Bugs, the Buddha of America,
faces off as we hear,
"Om-m-m."
"Ehhh, what's up, Doc?"
"Om-m-m," again.
"Can you believe 'dis guy?"

Bright enough for light to bounce off my
turquoise gloves, Buddha's yellow jacket,
Bugs's red raincoat. Last quarter mile big hill
suddenly flattens out
and I fly home.

RICHMOND BLUES LOOK YELLOW TO ME

Too poor to grow up in Richmond, broke enough to
work there a month: its houses—"herses"—
gracious, even modest neighborhoods, treed,
grand and span two or three centuries.
Sleepy, hip at the same time
like pre-commercialized pre-60s Texas.

Walks down West Side driveways, streets—
not a walking district, they use the malls—
through cemetery where John Marshall rests
with shy rock-and-roll, blues and jazz singer
and sexiest man in Richmond as far as I could tell.
"You have pretty eyes," then sang his song, "Josephine."

In front of 40 polite songwriters,
some sporting layers of sturdy George Jones hair shellac,
I sang "Ordinary Abstract Invisible Love"
to my friend Ed's cosmic-bubbling electric piano,
wasn't nervous till I noticed my shaking hands, still
I felt like Marilyn Monroe.

Drove 23 miles to Hanover schools to Sheila Chandra's
Indian-Irish-Catholic-Hindu songs,
breakfasted on rice pudding, spoon bread, or Greek flan.
Morrisons cafeteria for supper with discerning
new friends—their credibility unquestioned by me—
they dress up like clowns just like me.

Richmond blues look yellow to me.

THE WAY IN, NAVAJO MOUNTAIN, UTAH

Sprung into enviable vibrato by
red sand road—deep sand—insistent
in wash-boarding me into the chorus of
"The Circle Game" so many times more
than I want to even if I knew the verses and I know
every nut that caresses every bolt in the chassis
of my shiny white 4 X 4 the state of Utah has
entrusted to me is unscrewing, like in a cartoon,
shuddering with every bounce and buck of the road
as it occasionally skis toward the edge of a 60-foot
drop off the side and I try to decide on
first, second, drive or the brakes,
fully not yet ready for the circle.

SEARCHIN' FOR ANASAZI SLIM

Bouncing in out, out in deep, red sand ruts,
piñon and sage limbs scrape the doors, slow us,
snare, snag us off undulating trail,
stop us before we spin our wheels.

Gotta have a tape deck, gotta hear true grit
classic Smithsonian blues—Eddie Cleanhead Vinson,
Count Basie, Muddy Waters—in wild desert—
Elmore James, Jimmy Reed, Little Walter

bouncing along, four beats to the bar,
twelve bars to the song, bent notes,
harmonica breaks, baritone wails, shuffling trap drums—
until we leave the car, plunge into desert up, down

smooth-red-sandstone-round-rock islands that dot
crypto-valley three miles from the Indian school:
no Park Service designation, no interpretive signs,
no hot dog stands, no fees, no cars—except ours—

no people, except us, no sounds, just echoes of a
crow and Joe Williams yodeling how often he gets the blues.
Up on lost mesa, we say "yaa'teh"—"hello, walls"—
walk around red-, gray-rock-rampart remains,

where way up here in the weather—sun, snow, lightning—
they gasped, sipped lemonade on their front porch,
gazed out over 60-foot drop at canyons, washes, reds, blue-greens,
and listened to Anasazi Slim's latest hits.

CASING HYAKUTAKE, MARCH 27, 1996

Sherron the innkeeper shames me into this—
"You're going to write about the comet, aren't you?"
Second night of second week in second school,
fourth week in her rooms, I luxuriate indoors,
too cold out when I can just peek, mist
up the recycled windows in the new barn—
less misty than 1996 recycled tail, test
driven every thousand generations,
upstaging razor-edge moon,
20-year-kilowatt Venus.

Last week we looked and looked for it
south of east over crescent wooden bridge
into neighbors' yard just as they drove in,
have we snagged all their treasures?
All we knew was we were shivering—
she in Russian tweed jacket, me, flimsy flannel shirt—
"Is that it? That piece of lint?" we sighed,
cold, disappointed, as the neighbors eyeballed us
back around the corner of Ephraim, Utah,
back down the handle of the same dipper the pioneers drank in.

OM-ING IN WYOMING

St. Patrick's Day six or seven of us
squat-sit shivering along
the grass-high hedgerow garden beam—
it's too cold to be outside
but inside is too warm, too
comfortable, drunk, republican, safe,
too much unreturned eye contact, smiles, hi's—
so we sit out here on the edge under
the full Worm-Crow-Full Crust-Sugar-Sap Moon,
the altered class, letting go
of our voices so they can
mingle with the stars over the mountains.

SAP

The first day of spring came my 50th year
the first Sugar Sap Moon quarter
and changed my life into a river.
I scuff through two-day, two-inch snow dust
to massive triple Shiva of a cottonwood,
titan's (eagle's) nest—built of branches not twigs—
installed on third floor. Under and around and around
I look up the trunk of the solitary grandmother,
tramp across suspicious snowy bogs that
hide riverways and creak as I cross
powdered ice that doesn't give way,
walk the last meadow where the hills
rise up gently on both sides like waves,
the golden dogs running up and down,
until I come to a crossing too big,
too deep, too flowing for a ford.
I hug the edge like the thick, flat icebergs
that crept somehow up the banks below
to a fallen log where I sit in the sun,
watch bluebirds feed on Rocky Mountain
plankton in melting-creek-bank platters,
and wait and wait for them to fly away.

MARRIAGE OF THE MONKS, A LOVE POEM:
DO YOU MEREDITH TAKE THELONIOUS?

No place like
a sphere of dissonance
as serene as holding an infant
where everything makes sense
where processionalists bear clouds on poles
where nursery tunes play in minor keys
where the music you used to hear in your head
has been layed down on sides—Bluenote, Riverside, Prestige—
is being sung on stage, "nah-nah-nah-*nah*, nah-nah-nah-*nah*. . ."
when your lower lip begins to droop
when the dots in the air become distinct
when you reach a state of equipoisal grace
when it all regains its fuzzy state
you remember the music you heard
in your head a long time ago
longing for it you're
home.

SNAKE-EFFECT LOWS: LESSONS FROM BOZEMAN, MONTANA

There must be some mistake: weren't you
my dream man—aging woods hippie-artist
with references in Helena, slew of guitars,
mandolins—was that a double bass in your
living room or were you just glad to see
me?—Texas-fiddle tapes, beat-up V-dub bus,
the right books—Gary Snyder, Jaime de Angulo,
Lao-tzu—sublime lines: "I learned a new
instrument every time my heart got broke."

In your fuchsia four-door Alfa Romeo
you Romeo you said you swapped for a dobro
revving like a flat-bed rubber burner
from Gillette, Wyoming, drowning out sexy
Shostakovich public radio letting us make
only right turns because if we didn't the left
front wheel growled loud threatening to fall
off if we went left, our route to and from
the pizza place taking us lazily all over
Bozeman—you, me, and the woman you rented
a room from who had a crush on you. Like a
d.j. you whispered, "Stick around."

Nearly fall. "Today's Hank Williams' birthday."
Boy, you laid it on thick—it was really two days later.

The lessons:
1) I believe anything
   a smart, funny man I'm attracted to
   tells me.
2) I'm hyperactive and batty.
3) Never tuck in the blankets.

HEAT

The following have been known to
give my hormones pangs: tentativeness,
feet, the perfect arcing line of a beard
I once knew just below the cheekbone,
walnut-brown eyes, a lope, a yodel, a burr,
hazel eyes, a custom-made mandolin.
Smaller things than these have tripped,
trapped and tried truncated me.

What set me off this time? My swallow's
clammed up, warmth shoots down and out
my limbs, pressure on my chest, waves of
bliss ebb and flow through my arms and legs,
neck, head and torso—to say
the word *body* seems too suggestive.
All this from little estrogen molecules?
from some musky bombshell?

Riding in cars with certain throbs I've gone
limp in the neck, passenger seat embraced
me, let my head drift, drop back and back,
caress the top of my spinal column or
the flex of my foot, wiggle of my toe,
swipe of my tongue over my palate and
lips, the juice in my ligaments become
world capitals of sensuality.

Today every tree acts like a conspirator,
gesturing limbs, snickering leaves,
all the while pretending to stand
deaf, dumb, blind, and still—
no wonder I want to be one.
A breeze soft enough to squeeze,
ripples on the lake like oil paint,
pillow clouds will be gone tomorrow.

LAUGHING ONE AFTERNOON

I run down a 30-foot grass-dusted dune,
soft Duck Harbor sand flies, my dog
Charlie jumps, barks at my side—
bright sun wind-music beach day—

My best street chemistry
has always been with dogs so this
three-p.m. intimacy comes as no surprise:
look into my eyes they say, they all say.

ECSTATIC

Falling on a Sunday morning for twenty-four hours
or a year for smart, funny artist next to me
from Fife in Virginia black Baptist church takes
an hour and forty-five minutes, maybe less, maybe
from the minute the choir slowly two-steps
down the aisles singing "Hard Fighting Soldier,"
pierces through me, reassures me so I might have been
at Crow Fair pow wow back in Montana,
the light moves forward and back and forward, en-trancing,
the light behind the blue and yellow
stained-glass windows blaze brighter,
the pastor rings out on *community*
and the walls and floor and ceiling and windows rock,
and he, next to me, sends out burred gamma waves
that travel on spiny sighs.

DAWNSPRING

It is dark and still as the night
lightens to impressionist
robin's-egg blue-gray and the birds
suddenly go off like someone's
inner beauty rising like a sun behind
lateral clouds sneaking up and up
until you turn around and there it is
shining in your eyes.

FALLOW

After you left I was rescued by two
women and a mustard field hanging just in
front of blue-haze range, the mustard
picked its spots in two-foot-high clumps,
red dirt line of a field hovered,
quiet with old corn stalks, above the road,
triangles of an alfalfa field and forest
foothills looped down toward each other—
the lines of angulation gently lapping
into each other at thirty degrees—all
foreground for low-slung ridge, which
opened the sky up even more than seemed
possible or tolerable now at low tide.
"Now look at the colors," one said,
"see what's going on here."
"You can't use green or brown," said the other.
Healing on a hill as the hours tick by,
sitting here with my paper and pastels on my knees,
my throat full, stomach empty—
I know what it is I do best.

RIGHT TO A LIFE

On slow spring mornings or windy
I walk in the slow but sure true
gait to where I can write this,
under apricot-front-lit gray clouds—
through direct slats of enlightenment
drilling through cloud mound—the shy dog
dances after me, empowers me.
I enter a solid world of bird songs

just to break the code:
blue and yellow equals green, life, myth—
I'm blue, you yellow, the evidence shows
up in our clothes, in our new plantings
in haute rows, in places where surely
no one else would find anything
much less look.

YES (OH YES I'LL BE RIGHT OVER) SINGS THE WIND

We walked past ether-like wind chimes,
heedless of their warning, our arms even around
each other once or twice. You bought chimes just like them—
pricy, they sounded like a koto
and ran the third of an airline ticket
to somewhere I can't go.

We sat on the last afternoon
across a small table from each other—
it might have been an ocean—
eating two orders of sacramental
fries with ketchup in the
sleep-deprived section of Hardees
and you blurted out barely
above the din of our silence,
"Could you live in the East End of London?"
Stunned, tongue-tied, unable to think on my feet or off,
surely I must have said something before I let it—
the very idea—vaporize—some siren I am!—and then
if that weren't enough, I bought the chimes, too,
fearful of hearing yours, fearful
I'd never see you again or that I would.

CARRIED AWAY

Under overarched footbridge,
dangled legs and arms, Goose Creek
races, rushes away in eternal exhale,
sucks, drags drooping willow branches,
stray grass and dandelions to the Missouri,
shushes, gurgles, ripples, roars,
reflects blinding midday sky.

Slippery river rocks in hazy mid-afternoon gorge
laughed as we skipped stones across jade spring rush
but couldn't look at each other or speak
so you walked down river and I
sunned on a boulder by the rapids,
practiced missing you, and
watched the Maury on its way to the James.

If you can look at a river—
the course of it, the direction
it takes, the strength of its current,
the predictable breathing of its white-water
gymnastics, the clarity of its quiet waters—
and ignore the metaphors,
can you just look at it?

SHRUGGING OFF

The moon shrugs off the earth's shadow tonight
but it takes two full moons, eight packs of cigarettes,
three six packs, a bottle of brandy and
nearly a fifth of tequila to get over
you—over me—not that much not
counting the moons because what is it
if it's not self-indulgence—both of us
taking some responsibility, at least
share the burden—who started it, anyway?—
maybe next time think twice about
giving uninvited, altruistic hugs or
slinging arms around someone's shoulder—
maybe not—because when you're in it
you're stuck seeing the other
as a part of a shared whole—
you're not even seeing the shadow of the other
for your own reflection coming back at you—
indeed, the blinding stuff of love,
the other's emotional reflecting pool—
no wonder friends gasp, "Gee,
he's so much like you," although
one said I could do better—maybe so,
maybe in the rational days of yesterspring
I would have agreed and even known
what they were talking about.

MAY WAS, MAY BE

Thank you, late snowstorm—denier of lilac blooms,
delayer of cottonwood, yellow-branched willow
leaves, co-emerging tulips and peonies.
This action-packed May doesn't fly by—
longest of Mays—unsettled weather—wind
breathes in, out, east, west,
back, gray, back, forth,
clouds boil by to the north, south—
unable to make up its mind, my mind,
except in depriving rain, echoing me oh
except for the free-flowing tears
of self-pity centerfold flood plain.
Why can't real life be charmed?
How does love feed on the passions of the other
in swirling winds or calm?

THE TROUBLE WITH LIVING IN THE MOMENT

You held your arms straight out for me
as though I were a child, so I could place
mine around your neck and you wrapped your arms
around me, letting me in, taking me in,
hugging me harder, surer, snugger,
longer than anyone ever has and all
I had to do was submit, let you in,
give myself to you,
collapse in instinctive reaction of trust,
surrender, emit a series of sighs
that took a lifetime to learn
how to let go.
                    You could have
taken me to your cave, said or done
anything, and I would've gone along—
heart and being turned to willed putty—
It took as long as I wanted
to extricate myself from deep,
thrilling, inevitable embrace
right out of a Bergman movie.

SUBLIMATION

I brought home wind chimes that were guaranteed
to sound like the music of the gods, ringing
each time you thought of me—a friend's conceit—
but ever since I put them away
for the winter I've been pulsant
on a daily basis with intoning tears
that climb and descend the pentatonic scale.

MR. ADEQUATE

No hanging on his every word or
sighing at the very sight of him, I'm
down to the basics: any smart, funny,
snappy, iconoclastic dreamer I'm
drawn to who thinks I'm wonderful will do;
doesn't have to have an accent, though
Scottish or Texas'd be thrilling;
doesn't have to be tall, though six feet
would be a cute altitude; need he
dance? be nice, though he wouldn't have to
do Russian splits in air; I'd like him to
grasp my elbows passionately,
kiss my meandering zones regularly,
give me smiles like he was lookin' at a
hot-fudge sundae as often as possible;
no marriage, real-estate ventures,
just real adventures,
free rent in his arms.

MAYBE HE WAS REPRESSING SOMETHING HE WASN'T FEELING

Next to me at dinner you fingered the hem of the tablecloth
slowly, distractedly, the sad, strained look
in your face cut into me, too. Another day,
a day you said you felt bad,
I walked up to you and, beaming,
you did three consecutive Russian splits in the air—
as best you could.

We were, by turns, giddy and wrung
on mountain roads, by a river, in a K-Mart, and now
here I am, seven times zones away,
where I still watch you, listen to you, sense you,
wish you were another edge dweller, seeker of a charmed life.
But it's women not men
who fall into those categories, isn't that so?

MOONOPAUSE

It's 1:48 a.m. I wake up
unable to go back to sleep but
so does the whole town if gossip's the truth.
Years of formerly blissful sleep
spoiled, split, splayed by the change, spare change—
but still that doesn't explain the whole town.
Or is it the moon, the rationed water supply—
certainly not you though it's you who
fill up my wakeful gap—that burns this town's
candle at both ends, folks behind their wheels,
shopping carts, bank-teller windows dragging through
another summery week of sleep deprivation as
the moon sits only just past first quarter and
deftly sets a good two hours before we all open our lids?
Just because you have sleepy in your eyes in the morning
doesn't mean you slept; it just means you had
your eyes closed for awhile.

SPLAYED

in my hammock, eyes, throat ever full,
I act out my life as a bum, under flighty
leaves tatting test patterns against dark blue,
the hot August wind blows over me
through red, yellow, orange hammock strings,

galefully persistent, tugging, nudging me along
obediently to my next appointment, which,
keen on, I'm unprepared for—or maybe a missile,
like the grateful golf ball of a high-scoring novice,
embracing, relishing, mainlining all the stops.

I'D LIKE TO COME BACK AS A TREE

I'm waiting for the perfect moment,
the moment between the apex of breathing   in   out,
just before and after the beat that separates an old and new year,
but I'll settle for the final cutting of grass,
kids' new squeals in schoolyard recess,
collecting cosmos seeds, September crisp-heated
breeze, dodging drunken bees that zag zig fast slow
round legs, arms, face, wind chimes,
sway the final hour of summer in hammock
beneath transient robins, warblers, chickadees,
happily heart-broken-open one minute,
soaringly ethereal the next—
the dance steps before, during, after the love state,
cha-cha chakra number one? two? three?

Now all is quiet, no movement, no sound.
Numbness? indifference?
A stillness signifying some serenity?
I pride myself being easy, detached—
it is all the same to me, bodhisattva-in-training—
but this is disinterest, shutting down,
closing off, cutting out.

                                                Is severing

the imbecilic umbilical Gordian
cord of desire what the gods
require of me for their having
scooped me up, held me in a giant
hand for the five warm months, carried me
along in the world, beveled all the sharp
edges so though there was ache there was no blood,
eased me through a soft-focused,
sweet-scented, joyous world

                                              until now
as they descend the hand to the ground, gently open
huge fingers, nudge me out, and just like that,
I'm left to move through the world on my own again?

WHERE NO MAN HAS GONE BEFORE

When love meets creativity,
that moment when possibilities
from cataclysm to engenderment
run thicker than water,
I want a tractor beam to pull out
my heart from my clutches, so busy
breathing in, reading reality—
"What's so great about reality?"
the best line in the movie *Lilith*—
zeroing in, more in touch
with your feelings than you are,
turning me into a kind of Cassandra—
each time I tell how it is,
it's shrugged off as a joke,
each time I try to kiss
off my fervor it grows deeper,
like the Enterprise's phasers
trying to destroy some alien
anomaly that instead of dying
gets stronger, more intense
with each devastating blast—a defiant
Cassandra calling shots
no one will claim to have fired.

INFLUENT

Never thrown myself at anyone before
much less hurled over an ocean—just when
do I land and, now that I've dropped my compass,
where? And if love's not about possession but
surrender, does it mean that I'm now
self-destructive, self-obliterating, generous—
does it really matter what I am?

Every night I go to bed in the hope
of waking up having arrived somewhere
but instead I'm still circling, unable to move
my legs, my arms frozen in an attitude of openness:
I knew I was going to get waylaid
but did I know I was going to have to try
every day to map the way in?

"I feel like you're in your real heart today,"
a friend tells me, calls me Narcissa now,
listens to my confused aerial geography,
looks me in my formerly innocent eyes,
wet eyes from heart-displacement overflow.
If this is my real heart, do I have enough of it
to get to the heart of it and out again?

EMBRACEABLE

(after a painting by Edmond Tarbell, "Across the Room")

The air is so clear I can see
the pigments in the floor dissemble
into browns, pinks, greens, sienas,
so still the canvas lies forgotten and draped
over the arm of the sofa, no breeze rustles
by or enters the slats of the shutters.
The white dress is surely heavy, hot, envelopes her
as surely as the room is nearly empty,
as she tries to recline, recover her ability to live
here, in this room, hampered
as she breathes in the roar of the wind
from a mountaintop, distant, close as a dream,
encloses her like a final hug—
much deeper than a mere hug—
able to sigh, unable to breathe,
unable to think of anything else.

TRAVELING DAUGHTER

Long ago in a small self-contained fertile valley,
a beautiful young woman caused every farmer
in the land to turn his head and fall in love with her,
but not one followed the young woman. Instead
they watched her from the confines of their corduroy land,
as she walked across their fields against the grain.

How many years, how many furrows do I have to
step over? she asked, picking her way across
the dry, dusty-gray elongated mounds that betrayed not
the smallest sign of life, not one iota of trust,
walking across the unending fields of I don't know
how many acres, furrow after furrow,
never arriving at the forest, the pond, or
wherever it is that hope lives.

WALKING AROUND WITH YOUR EYES CLOSED

The mountains hang blue and thick
in the near distance—sometimes
the haze usurps the view
like a fickle set decorator—
nearer, redbud and dogwood blooms
nearly burst off their branches and
too lush smells smack the air
and anyone on the path lined with boxwood.

People accuse me of never working.
I am, sort of. Always walking
around in the quaint gentle safe air—
a golden opportunity—or lying in
a hammock so deep between two trees
that occasionally rock so palpably
when the roaring hill-topping breeze
picks up, the inland feeling turns
into a longing for a life preserver.
A perfect trust more luxurious
than a limousine to a city girl.

PRACTICE

Up until now—shaken, splayed—
I've led an exemplary life. Now
I have doubts about the very air
reaching for the core to heal
my wound and applaud the water
pouring out of my eyes like healthy melting
snowpack. No riding lessons
this time to buck the fear—
no diversion dam from your *couer.*

My last damn diversion—just another section
of impossible kite string that measures
not length or height but depth—
surrender made visceral, spiritual.
Friends assure me that it's just fine,
"it's practice," until, they imply,
the real thing comes along,
but I doubt any of it is practice at all
and not really the real thing.

SESTINA FOR JEREMY BENTHAM

Steep snowy tricky trail trips me on my side in pain,
left ski at nine o'clock, right-angled from my knee,
sharply twisted tendons, hamstring, I see a ceiling
of dark blue slip through the pines,
try to rewind my ski, my knee between throbs—
I pass out over and over, second by second.

I rub the knee neighborhood a second
to see where my leg emits pain,
slowly get up between throbs,
careful, no weight on that knee.
A limp breeze push-pulls branches of the lodgepole pines
as I limp a mile back under crisp cobalt ceiling.

I watch the fan stir warm air off the ceiling,
often what passes for an hour is really a second.
Way off the mountain, no forest of pines
comforts me on my couch of pain,
two bags of frozen peas brings my raised knee
grateful numbness between throbs.

The flu comes, too, clogged ears channel dull throbs,
no balance, I land face up, knee bent under me, under the ceiling.
Hyperflexed, the therapist says, my pre-sprained knee.
Had I been hurting before? In a second,
a new, enhanced round of agony and pain
leads me to pray hard for permanency beneath the pines.

Hobbling on upside-down ski poles erase the pines
from my mind—hard enough to reach the fridge between throbs
much less try to *om-m-m* away the pain
or mandala-ize soft, slow fan-blade blur near the ceiling—
I imagine not hurting, if only for a second;
down and down, unswelling, the left knee

slowly comes to resemble the right knee.
If I were really a strong woman, I'd live in the pines,

but I live in town, minute to minute, second to second.
I am independent—no dates or heart throbs—
I know the real stuff of life is under the skin, above the ceiling,
and that the absence of pleasure is pain.

How much pain can one knee take?
How high a ceiling can the pines make?
How many throbs into each second break?

AS A DROP OF WATER FLOATS ON THE OCEAN IN THE PATH OF AN ONCOMING SHIP

Only ten minutes ago I lay
in bed hoping to drift off quickly
before I had time to get started brooding
when before I knew it I was laughing
and crying at the same time, receiving
some kind of hallucinatory caress,
my body obliquely wrapped in warmth,
and before I could speculate on
the origins of this phantom enfolding
it dissolved into my skin.

RIGHT THROUGH YOUR FINGERS

I found a way to avoid traffic
jams at Interpersonal and Vine:
all I have to do is open the trap
door beneath my feet and I'm out
of there, falling effortlessly,
fearlessly, no destination, not
even down, no parachute needed—
I can come out of it any time
I choose—no more strife, the quiet
life listening to the birds go off
just before the radio goes on,
hours after I lay awake hours
sobbing my way out of town getting
up to let go of a poem way before it
dawns like a hot knife through thin air.

SPIRITUAL SCHIZOPHRENIA

"A change of place is mere transportation; a change of heart is action."
                                                  Sri Nisargadatta Maharaj

Passing squall lines churn the Gulf—
chew up the beaches, throw up foam
so like gray ice chunks onto the seawall
I forget where I am and swerve to miss them.
Pourdown days at Jamaica Beach and South Jetty,
grateful ibises, cranes, pelicans—
where do great blues go in a maelstrom?
Flood tide surges energy through me,
up, down chakras 1, 2, 3, *and* 4.
All because the year's closest moon
waxes behind the mists
or is it really just menopause?

Were it his way, my guru would beam:
uncompromising, artless, honest blurts
of love blow over my ex-lover innocently
sipping a beer in a booth at Sonny's Place—
"Aren't we blowing something special?"
"You really still want me"—how low can I go?
Tantrums, bounded by no propriety,
at last, I get to live out high school:
I stalk, tail his red Mazda truck at high speeds,
break and enter and phone,
hang up stunned on my replacement.

No beach, no pride, flood tide.
Hazy sun glints off palm fronds in the backyards.
Refuge from the wind, the gulls glide in.

PITCH

Country boy act works on me,
so does singing together—
sound of his voice, mine following
in slipstream, drawn into harmonic dance,
soft curving cosmic waves—cosmic because
they refer back to me—stream in, out.

Each day the thing gets bigger
in me, anyway—I'm such a sap,
but then I've got a hole in my heart—
a word, a phrase, a touch, a jostle,
eyes and smiles, my air growing giddier.

"You're about six times faster than me,"
he drawls, slow and deep. He doesn't know I
want to go slow, want to come back
a ponderosa pine, which he already is.
I want to sing with the wind through his branches.

WHY WOULD I WANT

a passionate gentle smiling Southern boy—
Tidewater or Dundee—to sing with—
our vibrations warping and woofing
strands of translucence around us,
ethereal, palpable, comfortingly dopaminal,
climbing into each other's spaceship hearts?

YELLOWSTONE FALLS AND SO DO I

("Yellowstone Falls," by Albert Bierstadt, oil on canvas, 1881)

The water flings itself over a saddle of taupe
uplifted rock, resulting river below spews up
pink mists to meet low-slung clouds that angulate
to form a peak in the upper center.
Two things strike me: the up and down roaring
escalators of water and rock
and the light, oh, the light that lands somehow
in the canyon on all sides at once—
not impossible in a Bierstadt painting or a heart.

Good old Al, who went out West on 1200 migs
of 19th-century LSD and a sack
of money from the la turista-hungry railroad barons.
Still I love the golden late afternoon
wonderland air created by gravity,
luminosity, reflection, refraction.
Oh, to be one of those spindly lodgepoles
that cling to a boulder-strewn shady incline—
or maybe a cutthroat going over the falls,
letting go at 90 miles an hour,
60 feet per second, fins over head,
tail flashing on the way east through the West
under pinnacles that catch the sun from impossible angles—
that's what they said about constructing the railroad—
or red Indian paintbrush in tricky bottom
left-hand corner, and the trees look Japanese.

Stand close but not too or risk ruining
the psychedelic-ness of each drop of oil.
How long did it take the Yellowstone to fall?

SUSPENSION OF DISBELIEF

Mayday-urgent side channel
bleeds into the dull gray river
from distant red canyon—
split river flows unmerged
til red river takes over—
next county cloudburst
scoured red-topsoil rush
into palpable gush—
Filling Up Canyon Way.

Do Athabascan bible stories echo
our horror, shock, and dread?

Datura gods, great blue heron guide smile.

Then, we see it—the red hole—
looming six-foot waves
roar from liquid-sienna mouth—
we take out, line canoes around
rocks, red mud, stunned,
paddle on down the San Juan.

MOTH WINGS

Moth wings beat in my ear day and night
scolding me or leading me out of my life?
I breathe deeply and let go of the fight.

Deep hum--train? fridge? chakras not quite right?
oncoming stroke? karma of insurrectionist ex-wife?
Moth wings beat in my ear day and night.

I grasp for sleep, lose the battle to the light
of the dawn, my energy spent on strife.
I breathe deeply and let go of the fight.

"Go someplace, like Castaneda* did"—right!
Sever your synapses with a mental knife.
Moth wings beat in my ear day and night.

How do you not mind your mind? sit tight,
learn how to be, live from the gut like wildlife.
I breathe deeply and let go of the fight.

No mystic, I must sit with courage and with fright,
waiting for the dawning of my true life.
Moth wings beat in my ear day and night.
I breathe deeply and let go of the fight.

*Carlos Castaneda–His real, hallucinated or made-up depictions of his
purported study of shamanism are riveting.

THE BOY GENIUS IN THE COMPUTER LAB SAYS, "EVERYONE WHO COMES HERE WRITES A POEM ABOUT HEART MOUNTAIN."

A bird of pray circles Heart Mountain
for hours—it's always in your sights—
at the summit is there a sign, "Metaphor, elev. 8200 ft.?"
It's familiar terrain:
the bottom of an inland sea.

Breaking mountain ring encasing Sunlight Basin,
we breakneck downhill before we know it
going too fast, have to brake—"Road Damage"—
turn back north, east, then south, west, in, out,
break open a mustang heart.

When the hole in a heart expands so
the walls won't hold,
leaves love's lying, exposed outcrop—
magma's true confessions—
cured by the air,
utterly surrendered.

SEVEN BLURTS

When you have bad feet
you have good shoes—
lots and lots—all over the floor.

My friendships keep cratering
my will keeps revising:
I have many more shoes than friends.

How much starch and sugar
can be ingested in one day
seems to be the experiment of the week.

Seven coincidental occurrences
have come to pass in seven days—
must I wait for eight?

Eight, nine, ten and eleven,
the underappreciated last four sins:
boredom, smugness, worrying, complaining.

Figuring out guitar chords
by listening is so much more
pleasing than being told the wrong ones.

My friend shunned me in February
and by April my car broke down
and the whole world gave itself to me.

SIX QUESTIONS

Why try to be bigger than you think you are
when you're supposed to try to be
as big as you are?

Isn't it a pity
for it to be a dangerous thing
to think you're understood by a man?

Could depression be a bad marriage
where one's true self vanishes
as you robo through the motions?

How to rinse such a slippery slimy brookie
much less pan fry it so it doesn't
curl into the letter C?

How do you feel the love-ski
while slivers of multipartite
shrapnel whiz past?

Why does it have to be shame
that powers my revisions?

SMALL SALVE

So relaxed and snooping in laptop cockpit
while chicken sitting with wi-fi, I clicked on
my Dylan-groupie ex's post about Bob
and lo, a flabbergast paragraph jumped out
directly and subtextually at me:
"oooh!" at first, so stunned, so night watchman about
the facts which by evening didn't matter half
as much as my sleazy smug assumptions that
his discomforts linger and his quest for hip
that went out with 1965 lives on.

LONGING DISTANCE

I'm old now, you know.
One day I looked out the window and
saw something very large in the pond.
It splashed around a bit, captured the notice of
a couple dozen geese and ducks at the other end, and
two local wild dogs—not really wild but unschooled—
barked and howled and left just before
a deer emerged from the water.
He began to shake himself just as
another ill-tempered dog showed up, and
forced him back into the pond.
Have you ever heard of a deer swimming?

Her voice trembled.
It's hard to imagine her still
driving to Dutchess County every weekend,
driving back in city traffic. For three years,
nearly my total employee's health-insurance allotment,
I watched her aloe plant coil on the window sill
three stories above Central Park, our wilderness,
three times a week, two, one, then none,
trying to map my spiral.
I called to tell her I was self-actualized.

I said, I'm living proof of your healing powers.
She said, I'm living proof that I'm alive.

SHOULD I PUT ON FRESH UNDERWEAR? ASKS EMILY

Along the Bighorns, Wyoming's apostrophic range,
Monday, the last day of March, 2003, waxes weird:
Bad drivers, queasy stomachs, fuzzy heads,
muted steel-gray sky, thick snow-dirt dust
swirls up, down, left, right into evening headlights.

That morning, they began tearing up Main Street
two blocks at a time;
if the economy doesn't worsen or it turns
out this Iraq war was a good thing,
they'll probably finish it; otherwise,
it'll be Mad Maxx Rodeo Days every day.

By eleven, a sky-long, diagonal town-roof cloud
allows sun on the mountains but hangs
over us still at one, two-thirty, five, six-thirty.
How can a cloud not move? I wonder all afternoon.
As night kisses the cloud,
I pray they've come to rescue us.

JUST LIKE SPAGHETTI

In early spring, the golden willows billow so,
larger than the sum of their leaves, stems,
mounding, mushrooming branches
explode in explicit slo mo,
rooted, yellow-green clouds hang and thicken in
suspended animation for weeks
in the temperate river valleys of western China,
where they watched with impatience these subtle
phenomena and directly discovered
that gunpowder produced the same visual effects
only faster and ever since
little boys love to blow things up.

WATCHING THE WATER SPRINKLER

shower the grass with soft drops,
emanates, effervesces
spiral patterns late-day sun
backlights horizontally

OH HAPPY DAY

The end of the Mayan world
creeps into my brain—
it's on the radio—
rain today—around here,
the beginning of the world.
Twelve, twenty-one, twelve, is
that the date? It could be today—
I'd rather wait.
Open the windows, open the doors,
this is the ending I'm hoping for.

LOOKING AT THE SKY

long enough reminds me
we're not in charge
down here where why
would we know what we see—
stars and planets or the eternal brightness
shining through holes in the tent of heaven,
anger or hurt.

BE PREPARED

This [daily life] is nothing. This is like the Democratic Convention compared to true, deep reality.

Under the darkest possible blue sky
near and distant mountain snow blinds you,
be prepared for nausea, the dizzying, high-frequency,
silent music of the spheres that
whirs in your ears, your shallow breath that
catches at this inhumane altitude, while
your whole body pulsates in universal sympathy.
It's no wonder we chop wood, carry water.

Joanie Puma was fortunate to have inhabited a sheltered corner of the New York publishing world of the 1970s and '80s—a niche at *The New Yorker* she was encouraged by William Shawn to define and occupy—and fortunate to have realized that even though it was fabulous, she was niche averse. This notion was reinforced at the Virginia Center for the Creative Arts and Blue Mountain Center in the Adirondacks. Growing up on the sandbar that is Galveston, Texas, she imagined mountains in the sunset clouds, so when she dropped out at age 41, she headed first to the Blue Ridge and then to the Rockies. She's hiked and skied; her plays have been produced; she taught for the first time (for the University of Virginia's Young Writers Workshop) and traveled the country teaching and giving readings, including on the Navajo and Rosebud Sioux Reservations; her canoe capsized twice on a 63-mile river trip; and she is volunteer classical-music concert promoter for her local arts council.

www.ingramcontent.com/pod-product-compliance
Lightning Source LLC
Chambersburg PA
CBHW021156090426
42740CB00008B/1118